The Heart of a Woman

Jennifer Oneal Gunn

VIGILANTE PUBLISHING

Vigilante Publishing Group LLC
PO Box 668
Scottsdale, AZ 85252-0668

Second Print Edition 2014

02/092014

Printed in the United States of America

Digital services used, Kindle and Smashwords.com

ISBN-13: 978-0692300633

Edited, formatted, and illustrated by Jennifer Oneal Gunn ©2014

**Collaboration Poetry 'It Is You' by Poets Jennifer Oneal Gunn and John Aaron Green © 2012

FORWARD

This is a mixture of love, pain, and all the other things in between; I hope you enjoy the entrance into my soul. This is only about half of how I have felt in my life about all the things that life has to offer us, good and bad.

Dedicated to all the people who currently and have ever had my heart.

Table of Contents:

The Lighter Side:

Love
From Evil
Traveler of Hearts,
Searcher of Souls
Fallen
My Love
Help Me
Oh, Lord!
The Kite
The Truth Revealed
Silence
Every Part
In September
Faith's Hand
Love is Pain
Dear God
Numb
Full Moon
Letting You Go
Thank You
Solitude (For My Son)
The Night
Closer Still
The Storm
Blood Red Moon
Spirited
Across the Sea
Ponderings of a Broken
Mind
Confusion
The Muse
Still Embracing the Night
See and Understand
Waiting
These Broken Wings
Dreams
The Rain
Reflections
I Dare You
True Strands in Time
Sunlight
Something New

Two Are One
I'm Yours
The Light
You & Me
Honesty
No More
Open and Shut
My Heart
Heart of A Woman
Looking For the Light
For You
Take Me
Written, shifting, rising
The Sky
Finding My Peace
Flames
It Is You

The Dark Side:

Shadows
I Don't Want to Die
Love I Thought We
Shared
Scars of the Oppressor
Regret
To You, that Deserves
Far Worse
Sadness
Before You Go
Poetic Soul
Darkness, Dear Sweet
Darkness
The Broken Angel
Failure
Die Please Die
Just Stop Already
Not Even Death
Holes
Burning Candles
Love, Pain, and Rage
The Bridge
The Darkness
Cherished Days
To Sleep
Take Me Home
Silence Be...

The *Lighter* Side

Love

The sun enriched golden days of warm happiness
The moon enhanced his eyes on nights of utter
passion
By the light of day or dark of night,
They were meant to be in love
The stars crossed and worlds collided
Now they see how their world was meant to be
It came all too easy in the silvery moonlit night
to them
The beauty of the entire world could be seen
from their door
In the world we could ask no better favor than
love
Love that comes honestly to us
That comes with eternity
Peace
&
Tranquility
Now in this Summer of Pain there is life
New life
Just beginning
For the time has finally come
TAKE CARE MY LOVE

From Evil

This day of retrospect
I look at you and see
What I did
I look inside you and see
I see your pain
I'm sorry if I hurt you baby
No one word has the power
To take away your pain
Nor do a set of apologies

On this day
I wonder how to fix this
And move on with
All our lives
And good times
Where did it all go?
I can't help the pain
To go away
From your head

My heart is in a vice
I don't know how
To un-break your heart
I can't do anything
For you
And you are so precious to me
So it hurts worse
Than doing nothing for your because
I've cried nights for years for you
What now my precious one?
How am I ever going to make it right for us?
On this day
In hard times
How to figure you out?
How do I protect you from evil?
How do I protect us all?

Traveler of Hearts, Searcher of Souls

Weary and forlorn am I
The traveler of hearts
The searcher of souls
The guardian of love
Fore I have been on a mighty quest of heart
It seems so far that I have been searching in vain
All that has been found so far are lost ones
With lost hearts and lost souls
So I search onward into the night
And so I travel on this quest of mine
Fore someday it will reveal what I seek
This long journey will someday end
Fore when the time comes
I shall be ready for it
Until then
I shall carry on searching for my love
Ah, there will come a day…

Fallen

Falling stars
Stolen dreams
Hearts abound
With many, many things
Fate failed us
Once more
We see doom
Dreams I'll never dream
Words I'll never say
And in hopes
To love you no more
No more pain
The rain will fall down
Forever over me
Even when
Twilight's moon does shine
To never feel again
To never care
To never cry
Healed will be my soul
To love no more
To also never feel so torn

My Love

Valiant of heart
Rich of soul
Blood worthy of many
And all who seek it
Power of old
Heart of stone
Cast aside
Your weary dreams
My love
Ascend a staircase of gold
Come home to me who waits
So patiently
For your sweet embrace
On long nights alone
Visit me often, as is your will
Take none other than me
These nights so cold
And wash your hands
Of the streets so bold
Dream of us
In your time of need
Save your precious heart
For Me

Silent are your kisses
Loud are your footfalls
Your heart beats slowly
Let not these Angels sing praise
Let not your vision wander
From me
The light shines most viciously
Around our very mortal souls
Love me forever
Don't look away
Too short is our time
Earth is only home for a while
Can I break the stone around your heart?
Make you see
In times we are apart
Love lives on in me for you always
Sweet words whispered in my ear
Words everyone will grow to hear
Passion does never truly die
Tomorrow you come to me again
On the long fragrant wind
I sigh
Love forever is mine
In my heart you entwine

Forever Mine

Help Me

A stitch in time
That's all we have
To look at these days
I find it harder
To find my joy
In these times of dread
Please God,
Make it come back again
Make my sorrow end
If not forever,
Just a little while
Help me find my smile
Though my soul is strong
I feel cold inside
Bring back the light
That went out
Remember God,
I have not forgotten about you
Or that you love me
I pray and desire
Your light, wisdom, and joy
In my heart again
Fill me with this life once more
I need it so...
Please help me to find some peace,
Comfort me and hold my hand...

The Heart of a Woman

Oh, Lord!

Thorns bear into your skin
Blood rushes from you
Like a streaming river
You cry out in pain
No one hears
They only laugh at your pain
Oh, Lord
How that must have hurt you so
To see them
Smiling fondly
As you hung there, dying for them

Blessed is your eternal soul,
That gave of thou self for us
How we should honor you so
And be thankful to thee
That you loved us all
Enough to die for us
Your children that you didn't even know
Your soul so pure
Your heart so great
Lord Jesus forgive us these mistakes we make

Let our souls be yours this day
And every day
Smile on us fondly out of love
We know you're waiting
To take us up above
The clouds so high
To our home in heaven
One day we will see you again
Our Father's son
And our beloved friend
We love you Jesus!

The Kite

No longer will I be your kite
Blowing in the wind
Your soul is grim
When you decide to finally let the light in
I will not be there
Because you have sinned
Much to your chagrin
I will smile again
Out here on my own
My OWN happiness reigns
No matter what you say
And when you see me smile
I hope you feel pain
To never know this love again
I am gone from you now
Only lonely you remain
No more is left for me to say

The Truth Revealed

Tempered spirits
Sacred souls
Hearts Bursting
Minds erupting
All things inside
Out of control
Need to learn
How not to feel
Someday
I'll be just me
Won't have a
Need for anybody
Everything inside
Will be just fine
Someday I will
Look inside to find
And then
The truth is revealed...

Silence

In silent repose I sit
Faded into the background
Listening, watching, waiting
Not here but here all the same
In silence I observe
Seeing all that goes on around me
Quiet not wishing to say or do
Anything that might hurt you
Silence doesn't mean
I'm upset or mad
It means patience and yeah
I might be a little sad
But silence is what silence is
I wait...

Every Part

I love you deeply
I love you madly
I love you with my heart
Every inch
And every part

I don't know what you're looking for
I don't know what you want anymore
I just know you're in my heart
Forever more

I love you deeply
I love you madly
I love you with my heart
Every inch
And every part

You are my soul
You are my sunshine in the dull
You are my dream come true
Oh, how I need you

I love you deeply
I love you madly
I love you with my heart
Every inch
And every part

In September

The air is turning colder
The nights are giving way
To the coming of the snow
The morning always sets with dew upon the
grass
The sun is bright and changing
The lights inside are growing dim again, my love
So many years without you
So many more to go
Even though you know
That after all this time
You were always there
Deep down inside

Breezes turning colder
Everything getting ready
For the coming of the snow
When we awaken to a world that's turning gray
The sun is changing
And the lights inside are growing dim again, my
love
So much time has passed without you
So much more time will pass
Even though you know
That after all this time
You are always there
Deep down inside

Autumn is upon us
Winter will be here soon
With these winds of change
You sing a different tune
My world is slowly turning to gray
And the lights inside are growing dim again, my
love
So many years without you
So many more to go
Even though you know
After all this time
You're always there
Deep down inside

Faith's Hand

The dawning of a new day,
A new age creeps in upon us
Can you see the light up ahead?
Some call it hope
Most claim it's an illusion
But a few call it Faith's Hand
And Faith's Hand is coming to reach for you
Good or bad
Our time is coming to a close
Most have already known it was near
This day will be set as spiritual
Some will just say it's a special day,
Although deep down inside you know better
Prepare for the day
This dawning will come
It will come when no one is looking
And the light we'll see will be our miracle
beginning
So take time to rejoice while you can
Time is growing short,
In Faith's Hand

Love is Pain

Love is pain
I live just to die again
Truly, truly...

Why must a heart break?
Why must my feelings you take?
Why must I be so unworthy?

I can love like no other can
But to me YOU are the bits at the bottom of the
bin
YOU are the one who's sinned

I used to think I'd die for you
But now I know the truth
It's your time to stew

Love is pain
I WON'T live just to die again
Truly, truly...

Dear God

God hold my hand
Give me strength to smile
Hug me tightly to you
Be my guide

I know that you
Are by my side
Help me to help myself
I need your light

Surround me now
And hold me close
I need my smile back
I need to laugh

God help me to help myself
You know me best of all the rest
It's in your hands
And I know you love me

Show me the way back
Up my path
Let not this momentary sadness
Deflect the goals you set for me

I am deep now in this sadness
Help me find my way
Hold me
Hold my hand and show me

I know I rarely ask anymore
But sometimes I really still need you
I will always need you
To guide me, love me, and hold me…

Numb

I want to know why I have to be the one
The one to be numb
I can't feel what I should feel
Am I broken I often wonder

I'm not searching for you
You poor soul
I don't want to know you
I can't handle you

Am I ever going to feel good enough?
I don't know
I don't care and I don't want to
Make it all your fault

Just because I'm wiser now
Doesn't mean this is resolved
I don't trust you
I can't love you

I'm sorry but
There is no way
You get to fill me up
With promises

I don't think you'll keep them so just don't
I have been down too many roads
Too many times before
Yes I know how it all ends for me

No more into the shadows for me
No more hiding from the light
Just your light
I won't go into it, so I'll be safe

No more mistakes
No more worries
No more heartache
So I am this numb person

How is it that I still function?
I wonder this sometimes too
Being broken
Feeling like I can't be fixed

Full Moon...

Full moon, bleed it all out to the stars

They hear you and they are listening to all you
say...

Sleep now and waken to all that is new...

Refresh your heart and all that is you...

Time lost can be reclaimed,

All you have to do is smile...

Letting You Go

Crush me and I bleed just like you,
Remember,
Humans all bleed
We wilt we die

Hearts overwhelmed with feelings
Things you won't say
I'm done asking
I leave you in your own pit of despair
And take consort to my own

Black, red, and violent thoughts
Swirl to the never-ending pool's drain
I see blue…oceans of blue
Tears I can't stop

I'm not angry
I can't bring myself to be
Too busy bleeding on the shoulder of my shirt
And dealing with the ocean's worth of sadness
pooled at my feet
Head down and eyes off somewhere else

It's not like it wasn't fun, at first...
Sorry I cared too much
I'm just deep I suppose
Not much to do now

Just letting you know
I'm letting you go...

Thank You

Smashed, shattered, broken
On the floor;
Something I used to feel,
Something that used to embody me...
Anger, disgust, abused
And fallen;
Ways I used to express
The pain inside...
Love, light, laughter
Over this anew;
Still rejoicing in joy
Is how I now feel...
Thank you for this renewal
Upon which new things happen
And changes for the better
Are worth it...

Solitude (For My Son)

Solitude is for much reflection,
Time to think of all things,
The more troubles the more silence I want…

When I have a heart broken,
Reasons unknown,
I want time to see it all in my head…

Mulling, and mulling of things over,
I think it all through
And try to see it from your perspective…

I always ask those fated questions,
Even when I know the answers,
I must be alone with my heart as well…

And as damaged and broken as I am,
I see it all,
Life isn't fun ever…

But instances of wanting it all to stop,
For life to seize and not exist,
Only you can make me feel that way…

As soon as it happened it was over,
But you should know,
I'm not done with it yet…

Hence the solitude…

The Night

I'm into the stars
And in love with the night
Twinkling sighs I stand here
Subjected to your darkness and your will

Passion in the clouds passing
I own nothing and worry less
You're always there
I never have to search you out

Hold on to impending forever
And just let it be as it may
Not as it were
Everything is fine

Trust in me to be there
And I will
When you need me
I will look for you

Even through impending storms
I'm here
I won't run from your thunder
And Lightning is beautiful

Smile at me with your moon
So I can see it
Bright and illuminated,
All your light showing

During the day while you sleep
I think of you
And when you fall upon us
I can't wait to see you again

My heart is yours
For the taking
So Nightfall
Take care and take flight

Be kind with me
And do come again
I will wait for you
When your darkness descends…

Closer Still

Can't wait to feel your warm embrace
Your kiss, your hands, your face...
Frolicking our days away
In meadows green
Looking at the sun

As I close my eyes I burn
Inside this fire grows
No more embers, no more dust
Empty days are over for us
I think as I hold you near

As I lie on a blanket of green
Eyes wide looking at the sky
Closer still we are here
Clouds passing us by
Hearts floating just as high

You turn and smile at me
Wistful in your gaze
I brightly return it
And kiss your lips
Unfurling emotions pent up inside us both

Hearts colliding
Smashing toward the center of each other
Melding together with the heat
And the passion those kisses
Holding each other closer still

The Storm

I hear the storm brewing outside my window
Giving cadence to the one I know is in your head
I hear it and I think of you
I wonder what to do

The rain outside reminds me of renewal
Not despair
The thunder tells me of passionate things held
inside
Coming outward for all to see

The lightning in your eyes
The fire still in your soul
Don't give in or give up your fight
Never let go

Orange skies outside my window
Winds blowing savage
Much like the storms inside you
Wild and seemingly unending

Fight your fight
Silently raging, pouring out the hours
Heal your head and your heart
So you may begin again, without the sorrow

Blood Red Moon

The night, quiet desolate and open
Blood red moon hanging in my heart
Soundless and motionless
Dripping unseen the languid tears falling down

Stars unseen by the night's overpowering faulty
moon
Broken inside and sputtering in pain
Alone in the sky
Wanting to remain unseen
But I see you nonetheless

In these fallen shades of dreaming age
I see and
You are not alone
Dip down moon from where you are
Be in pain no more

I will hold your hand
Guide you
Feel sad no more blood red moon
Show yourself
Be no longer a full sight unseen

Spirited

Spirited and free
I feel this
When you smile at me
Life's not bad
For you and me

My heart is open
Wild things come
Wild things go
And they all flow
Like a river over us

Splashing over and hitting the rocks,
Are my emotions…
The shore was once
Littered with them
And they were all bad

Now all I want is
For the spirit
Inside to shine
And I see it in us both
So much light radiating outward

Happy and free are we

Across the Sea

Two hearts across the sea
Will see what we see
And wish what we wish

Too many miles
Got to have our patience
And see where it all leads

I waited in the days
For a part of my very soul
To show me his smile

And now I feel whole again
I saw the light in your eyes
And you saw mine

My giddy girly smile I gave you
My laughter you own across the sea
A part of your heart I know I carry with me

My own heart is full and runs over
To a place I have never been
But hope someday to go

Ponderings of a broken mind

Road weary and sallow
No longer willing
But still feeling the shallow
The ends that meet never do
Meet ends sacred and hallowed

Falling, spirited down
I sit in wonder
What is this thing?
I ponder,
Sit still,
I wonder
Can it be?
No not for me

My thoughts say…
Silly girl don't you know?
Have you never been told?
Love will never be yours to behold
Will you never ever see?
It will never be meant to be for thee
When will you learn, it's never your turn?

How can this be?
It's oh so easy…

Confusion

Confusion
Living day in and day out
With this heart
Full to the brim
Running over in fact
But catching it
Keeping it from hitting the floor

My confusion lies in fact
With knowing your fears
They are what they are
And acknowledge them, I do
But you also know mine
Constrictions abated and fears aside
I'm forced to hide

Confusion
My love is deep
And for you to keep
Time is but an open window
With it comes all the light
No worries, no fears, no more…

Confusion…

The Muse

To me this my heart be stilled
Always filled
Not always said
But never misread

You, my muse
Release things deep inside
Things I used to hide
But my heart will no longer abide

Never is there a need
To not tell you all I want you to know
And all the while the wild seeds grow
I will always be open, heart and soul

Even as the flowers fade
My heart will not evade
The way it feels will remain

Even as the embers ashen ever so slightly
Still it glows in quiet repose...

Still Embracing the Night

The moon shines
Its perilous wisdom
Down upon
All who gaze
Up at it from afar

Tempestuous trimmings
Seen no less
From the darkened doors
I sit here
Waiting for your gaze and your wisdom

Stars falling down
Catch it
Bring to me
All that you know
I miss it so

Dreaming in the days
I miss my moon and stars
Still in love with the night
Am I
Transposed to the journey,
Wishing to be…

With the night
As always we were
In passing times
See and Understand

Blossoms on the gate
Vestiges of things
Unspent and unsaid

Blooming silently there
People can see them
But they don't understand

Petals bringing life
All things new
Brought out to see

Much like you and me
We hide until
Things be seen

In our world
No one knows
They don't see or understand

We know
It's our world
To them the unknown

Waiting

All this waiting
Can I stand it?
At times no
At others, yes…

I wait for you
To taste you
To feel your touch
To see you

Is it worth it this wait?
Yes, I will wait
For forever if I must
You know

These Broken Wings

These broken wings
Healing all the time
Spreading...

These broken wings
Feathered out and changing
No longer sad nor dripping in pain

These broken wings
Ready to fly into the blue
All because of you

These broken wings
Aren't broken anymore...

Dreams

Dreams hanging
On broken strings
Tied in knots

Thoughts flowing
Outward but silent
To all but me

Never do I get
To untie the knots
If I do dreams will fall

Falling dreams
Hit the floor of the abyss
To be spoken of nevermore

The Rain

Misty rain
Blowing on my skin
I, once again
Feel quite akin

Spirit speak
Pour out your eyes
I listen
All too willing to hear

I feel your tears
Upon my head
I feel like
I'm far from dead

Nourish the earth
Like you nourish my soul
Again, refresh me
Take me in

Reflections

In the mirror
What do I see?
Looking back at me…

I see, I see
I see me,
I am now and forever free

I see in the mirror
Scars and broken wings,
In the mirror looking back at me

I see, I see
I see me
I am now who I always wanted to be

In the mirror
I look and I can see
This person, this one who knew and grew into
this woman inside of me

I see, I see
I see me
This light, this smile, this new antiquated happy
me
I see in the mirror…

Things of old upon my face
Things the years cannot erase
I see a heart that is fairly charred
I see a woman who works very hard

And all these things I would not replace
Because they will never take the smile that lives
forever to fill that space

I Dare You…

I dare you…
I dare you to stare into the darkness
I dare you to spread the light
I dare you to look at the face of evil
And I dare you to fight it

I dare you…
I dare you to Will yourself whole
I dare you to stand on and be brave
I dare you to face your fears
And I dare you to fight them all

I dare you…
I dare you to open your heart
I dare you to love without thought
I dare you to give unto those who need you
And I dare you to see the beauty before you

I dare you…
I dare you to want your arms wide open
I dare you to whisper faith at one another
I dare you to rejoice about living
And I dare you…

I dare you…

True Strands in Time

Seasons change
Things change

We grow
And we never stop

As of now
We worry and it never drops

Tomorrow it all changes
Yet again

Much to our sorrow
Things can't be like yesterday

The dying of the darkness
Bringing us closer to the light

Wisdom of man
Closing in on us

Derived immature thoughts
Giving way to all that is not

No longer just wondering
About what is in front of me

A strand in time
That's all you are

A season that changes
Endless and unyielding

Changing like the wind blows
Leaving nothing in your wake

Nothing but heartbreak...

Sunlight

Sunlight in the purest form
Speaks volumes to my very soul
Destiny winks out all harm
It brightens me to my very core
Sees me, and all that lie in store
I wish and wonder
But never ask what it all may be for
I only know it's my plan
And I must 'go with the flow'
So I may see the sun again

Too many days spent worrying over the plan
When I could have been sitting in the sand
With thoughts a flurry
And hands unbound
I could have just overjoyed in the sounds
Too much did I remiss
Now all eyes my way for things I don't want to
miss

All that time spent in worry
Why did I not hurry?
Out the door
To a distant shore
To share in the laughing
To share in the sunlight
Destiny I do regret
Not knowing you sooner
Thus making a happy ending yet
So much more possible
I do admit

Something New

Morning whispers softly something new
Bonds unbreakable
Forming strong and true

Awakening things
I thought I knew
My heart is abound and overjoyed

Too much light
Overflowing that can't be subdued
No more living in shadows

Open to the world
For all to see
There are we, you and me

Two Are One

Two lost souls
Bent and broken
Found each other
Finally

Two minds
Lost in a sea of despair
Now together
Happy

Two broken hearts
Mending one another
With the love
That fills them

That is when
These two become
One

I'm yours

Put your arms around me
Whisper in my ear
Tell me all those things you feel
Look in my eyes and smile that smile

I love you with my heart
And feel it in my soul
Deep into the inside of me
My core is full, spilling out
Willingly abound, upon the ground
For the world to see

When you touch me it sends my heart
Fluttering sideways and into my throat
My hands belong to you
My heart, my body, my soul
Are yours and yours alone...
Until time stands still

I'm yours...

The Light

The light is brighter now
Shining now
A beacon bright and true
I love this light created anew

So much light
It's all I can do
To not look at you
And smile wide

Laughter, joy, and heartfelt tears
The light you give brings
All those things and more
Just what I've always been looking for

The dark no longer lives and breathes
Not when it comes to
You and Me
Openly seen...

You & Me

Hearts and souls entwined forever
Never lost or broken anymore
You're worth more than you know
And your love is valuable
And those who don't know it
They're fools
It's not your fault
You did nothing wrong
I love you and you have me
For forever my love

You have my heart
And it's as big and deep as the ocean
Be strong my love
We can make it if we try
Remember
We can fly
No longer on broken wings
My sweet man always
I'm flying toward the sun
I'll take you with me
Always—always in your arms

Honesty

No matter what I will love you
Life and battles and all
No matter where life takes us
And in the hopes we don't drift

Subtext, context,
A million big bright stars
The future holds only what we want it to
And nothing more

In the confusion and subterfuge
Of how things are melding together
I find it hard sometimes to see an end
To this seemingly horrid beginning

Somewhere out there will be that end and the
beginning
Of the path we want to see on the paved road
finally
Are you still willing to hold my hand,
As we walk that gravel road together?

Do you want this path not lain with gold?
I know I do and that nothing is free
Nothing worth having anyway…
So could you be honest and tell me please?

No More

When darkness falls upon you
Know that you have me
And I love you
More than you know
No more shadows to hold you back
Or keep you down

You love me
And you'll see
No more darkness
No more shadows
No more hurting and holding it in
You have me, heart and soul

No more being shattered
Bent or broken
No more feeling like
No one cares
If only me
You have love

Open and Shut

Open arms and open heart
Open thoughts and open soul

Razors edge to the paramount
Trappings that fill us and rise

These trappings we asked for
And people don't get them

Too long we've waited
To find what we have

In essence the things
No one understands in us

Our purpose is no longer
That of pleasing those but us

And love is what we have
Sought out this long and found

Thoughts of angst
Because you can't have us

Those thoughts need to
Just vanish on the wind

My Heart

Oceans deep and miles wide
My heart is yours
You take me inside
In your arms I hide
In your heart I abide

Heart of a Woman

The heart of a woman
Deep
Thick
Dripping with the blood of her scars
Falling apart
Mending back together
Stronger when pain passes
Filled with love
Even when she shouldn't
She still does
If only just because
Some women
Are truly filled
To the overflowing brim
With love

The heart of a woman
Can sometimes only take so much
Bleeding
Crying, dying inside
Before just a little spot
Forever dies

Lessons learned
She's strong
She knows what she knows
And still she heals
To love another day
To trust another soul
To hopefully not break hers
Completely
The heart of a woman
With death-defying feats
She learns to live again
For her and those abound
The ones she loves
Around her
Those scars do heal
And her heart does always begin again
Miraculous wonder
The heart of a woman

Looking for the Light

Conjuring smiles out of dark dusty places
Something I like to see on others faces

Mine are new
Mine are just for you

Take them with you on broken wing
Take them with you for just anything

Let my smiles light the way
Let laughter be in play

Fill your eyes with this knowing light
Fill your heart with the sight

Take them all with you, take flight
Come toward me, come toward the light

Fill your pockets with my light
So you may have it even on the darkest night

For you…

I want to see your eyes dance
As you laugh
I want to see you smile
When you look in my eyes

I want your happiness
As a part of mine
I want your arms around me
Strong and firm
My head on your shoulder

Smiles in my heart as well as my face
My arms around you in a return embrace
One day I will kiss your lips
And you will kiss mine

Two souls becoming enter-twined
Sweet innocent fire coming to the surface
Building and breaking on the shorelines
Awakening the ghosts within us both
Wiping away the cobwebs of the past

Making way for something
Something honest and new
Something we both need
And something we both deserve

Take Me

Feelings twirling in my head
Feelings I only explain as everything
I want to be held by you
I want you to have your way
All the way with me
Running your fingers through my hair
I want to touch you
I want to have you all the time
Inside
Unfurling the inner being inside us both
Breathing, sighing, breathing each other in
Caressing feeling and knowing
You're my lusty heart's desire
Feelings I am feeling
Baby, taste your pleasures
And have your way with me
Plunge deep into me
Feeling all our ecstasies
Run your fingers over me
Feeling me tremble for you
Wanting you, needing you
Kiss me all over make me feel your fire
Burn me baby
Take me, take me, I whisper softly…

Written, shifting, rising…

Landing in fields of clover
Drifting off in space above
Head in the clouds

Starry gazes one and all
Shifting
Rising
Saving all
Hope and fairy tales

Whispering imagination
Headlong into dreams
Floating on the air we breathe

Nothing is quite what it seems
Hidden and falling
All the stars
Shifting
Rising

Swallow us whole
Picture us gone
Into the moor of fantasy

Shapes
Shifting
Rising
Falling in our imaginations
Trapping images to the page

So much tougher than it seems
For all those who wish
To dream

The dreams of written penance
Fairy tales unfettered
Upon the stars
Shifting
Rising…

The Sky

Shower me with drops of rain
Show me the moon
Are the stars shining on us from the same sky?
Or is it wishful thinking?

Lay beside me looking into the night
Tell me what you see
Do the clouds move above?
Or am I imaging it?

The trees blowing in the breezes
Make such little noises
And as we are silent and contemplative
The world moves on around us

Moments of sweet pleasure
Simple and untangled
Slowly around us
Soft and gentle in the looking glass of time

Finding My Peace

Within me shines a light
Small glittering hope
Amongst the pain
It grows and diminishes
At will

Emotions carry me through this life
And my little light shines

My heart seeks peace
Joy and the shining light
To shine so brightly

To cut the threads once more
Sewing them back together once more
Seeking and trying
To find that peace within
And my bright light shining for all time

Two Hearts

Two hearts still burn
No longer a solitary soul
That never gives up easy
I can't just let it be
Two hearts still rage on
Fires burning into the depths of
Our souls unwilling to give in

Two hearts still bleed
This blood of feeling
Tempered through thoughts unyielding
Souls that might still need healing
But these two hearts
They still love
They still feel passion
That's held inside

Flames

Embers they burn,
Constantly inside…
Turning, smashing the ashes below,
Spinning instantly,
Whirling into flames again,
Bringing to life what never truly died…

The fire of many nights' past,
Wishing for nights in the future…
For my mind churning, in embers,
Wrath in my heart,
In the flames of a once vibrantly burning fire,
Fires that turned blue instead of molten orange…

Things inside,
Crushing my middle,
My very core, in my center lives something
otherworldly…
Wishing to be set free, wishing to be the fire
inside you,
Sometimes just wishing to be,
Yet the ashes stay in place,
Sometimes suffocating me…

It Is You

The aggression of my soul is love,
Nevermore will I be held down,
To the trappings of my mind.
Will I ever see my yearnings fulfilled?
Heart's desires of a shattered past,
Scarred and dead...gone.
I wake finding my heart still wanting,
For, it is *you,* through all my troubles fade.

© Jennifer Oneal Gunn
© John Aaron Green

The **Dark** Side

Shadows

Born in shadows
Life is chaos
Living in peril and doom
Despair my only friend
I wish for the light
I wish to see love and laughter
I wish to break free
Free of these shadows
Ones that always hang over me
In darkness I dwell
In a tomb
This vacuous pit is not where I wish to remain
To see the world
Its glorious wonders
To know happiness

To understand joy

I Don't Want to Die

Flower petals falling

Stinging, burning, bleeding, bursting

Crying out

"I don't want to die!"

Hearts bleeding out

Catching only spots referendum

Pleading

"I don't want to die!"

Suffering withheld

Minutes, hours, weeks, years

Time will yell

"I don't want to die!"

Love I Thought We Shared

For all those unspoken times,
For all those times that were loud,
For all the love I thought we shared,
All the broken vows we made…

All those memories turned to dust,
Floating on the wind,
Carry with it my heart and soul,
Made of paper, worn and battered…

Too many shadows whisper in your place,
Too many awful thoughts do they replace,
Ones of love I thought we shared,
Broken on the floor…

Some things were not meant to be,
Certainly not you and me,
But love is blind and so am I,
Still I look to the shadows for you…

I see nothing but gray light there in the corner,
I feel nothing but tears and blood,
All running top to bottom,
Wishing myself whole again…

Scars of the Oppressor

I'm cutting these manacles of the oppressed off
Tonight
You can't see them
But I feel them wholly with me all the time

You didn't win and neither did I the oppressed,
Repressed and depressed
The thing you turned me into,
It was not the real me
Only a shell of before, long years ago…

I was stronger once,
Before you
And I will be stronger,
After your memory fades from me
I will remember that I once loved a boy,
Not a man…

All those times
It wasn't like I wished it would have been
And spending all that time crying,
Trying to figure out why
Shame on you,
The oppressor,
For you are not valid in your contradictions...

Hypocrite!
How are you still breathing?
By the dear grace of God,
Something you don't believe in...

But you are just one of many that I've saved
Saved from the hands of others
Hands much stronger than my own

Oppressor,
Peddle your wares elsewhere
And fail, you doomed creature,
Black as night,
To stay that way forever...

Regret

Lurking in shadows I see the things that wait for
me
Death and destruction of my heart
A part of my soul is dying
Pouring out and bleeding on the floor
Charred and rancid forever more

I feel the light that was once in our eyes dying
out forever
Never to return
Love is faded and gone
Petals of roses, dead on branches,
Brittle and broken
Strong is now weak as my heart bleeds

No more words to say and nothing time will
delay
The dead light sinks lower now inside
I'm barely recognizable
As are you
I regret it all

The Night

In the night,
Shadows lurk and form in the corners
And cracks in the walls of a building.
The night gives way to wicked things,
Urges,
Impulses,
Temptations,
And Delights.
Blood pours from the pores of innocents
Like wine waiting to be captured.
Closer the wanton become
To the very hell they wish to birth and bathe in.

To You That Deserves Far Worse

Shackles and chains thrown on the floor
You don't own me anymore
I do your bidding no longer
Freedom is my master now

To hell with what makes you whole
I could care less that you linger in battlements
And your soul is black
Find someone else to torture

Finally throw me back
Into the river you say is so deep
Not deep enough with the awful company you
keep
I will not be swayed to take you back

You have a heart of ice
And a head filled with stone
Too stupid to see what you did own
And that you had a home

I hope you look all your life
And the next one you ask to be your wife
Turns to you and says, "Uh-uh buddy, not on
your life!"
It would serve you right you know,
You useless torturer of souls!

Sadness

Tears fall down and blanket me
Covering me
Inside and out

Sadness you never seem to truly fade
Even when I'm not looking
You're there hiding

When will you leave me for good?
Am I to live with you?
For an eternity

I can never escape you?
Even when I'm not looking
You're always there behind my eyes

Even in my happy hours
You live inside me
Waiting to be freed

When will you die?
Must I die?
For you to exit me?

Knowing life is long
I do not want you
Sadness...

Before you go…

I see you
No more
I feel you
No more

No longer do you own anything I am
No more
I see scant black dots on the horizon
No more

I know you
No more
I've been deceived by you
No more

No more
Lost time
No more
Broken soul

No more
Bleeding heart
No more
YOU!

Poetic Soul

Poetry, poetic

Pathetic soul

Cries, ripping apart

Vessels spilled,

Blood rushing to the floor,

Splattering into the cracks of nothingness,

That once used to completely permeate the
space,

But had laid dormant for awhile

As the blood splashes about

Dust stirs up

Reminding me of very old,

Very real wounds in my soul

Things I had assumed had healed

And time and actual love were evident,

No that will never be, so,

I'm damned and tortured

Burning on my spit

Living yet again in Hell

Where I will always belong…

Darkness, Dear Sweet Darkness

I pray thee,
Take me in
Suffer no more
Heart broken
Mind sore
Toes tipping the edge
I see the bottom
Black
Lifeless and dispirited

I fall and see nothingness
I hear nothing
And want for nothing
Just nothing
But an earthly grave
With the silent shadows all around me
Peace, my mind is weary
I can never make it up

I can never pay it back
Or make it better
Nor can I undo my own heart
Sleep forever the emotions I didn't want to feel
Sleep forever the promises
Sleep the truth and the light
I can't see it anymore

Build a temple on one lie
A soul crushed beneath
Suffocating and dying
No flowers to grow in the wake of that one lie
No more to dream
No more with the lie and the line crossed
The hearts broken forever
Dead
Trust gone and forever missing always

And So...

And so the distorted life breaks
Beating on the shore
Tearing the vestibule of hate
Ripping at my heart
Appendages torn wide open
Bleeding emotions
Love seeping to the floor

The Broken Angel

This what I have felt like for a long time now it
seems,
My heart in sorrow,
My wings,
And my mind,
Broken.

Along with a lot of my heart,
The joy,
Smiles and laughter,
Gone.

I've lost things I can't get back,
I've lost parts of you,
Parts of my own soul,
Things I long to see,
But cannot.

Whispers,
All I hear,
All the noise is loud inside me know,
All I want are those sweet whispers to return.

Where is that calm of someday,
I wished for so many nights,
I can still hear it,

When you say it and I still want it,
But not if means,
Being so lost now.

I want you,
But I want you happy too,
With or without me,
With or without my heart,
So lost now.

With these broken wings,
How do I find my way again,
Back to before?
Before the sorrow and the pain?

And how do I help you see,
Maybe there is a better world,
Without me?

Just maybe you'll find your smile?
I will fight to find mine again,
Just can't see it now,
Don't want this fight,
Things are hard and,
My love,
Don't want you struggling.

My heart will always be yours,
No contest,
You have it,
Even though I know,
I don't have yours.

But you must,
I will be here,
In the time when you need me,
Right now,
You don't.

No dying,
Only breathing,
That's all I want you to do,
Keep breathing for me,
No matter how broken we both may seem.

One day,
Touch the light again,
See me,
Waiting for you,
With open arms,
Attached yet again,
To my open heart,
Ready.

FAILURE

My heart fails me

Yet again

Why's this a big deal?

I suppose it's not

Walls came down that can go up again

Boundaries set once more

And lines drawn

Cold and alone

This is how it must be…

How could I listen to something so broken?

Why did I listen to it, my heart is misguided

You shattered broken piece of junk metal why do
I ever listen to you?!

I hate myself so much for listening to you!!!

I HATE YOU!!!

Die, Please, Die

Why do I want to kill you?
Why do I want nothing more than to see you
bleed?
I want you on your knees begging me not to end
you.
After I've drained you of most of your life…
I want your useless corpse in my basement under
my floorboards
I want to know you're rotting

It all started out good then you made one huge
mistake
One that I have yet to forgive you for
I want to kill you
I want your useless blood on my hands so I can
smear it all over you
I want you to scream
I want you to die

I want to hold you by your hair
As I cut your throat
For what you did
I will never do it
You deserve to suffer out in your life
For who you are

Hell is too good for the likes of you
So I will not send you there too soon
Karma, asshole, will visit you
I don't care if you live or die
But I won't kill you
Half of me really wants to end you

My blade is too good for you
I wouldn't waste the time it takes to kill you
Lord help me, I want to see you fall at the hand
that deserves to do the job

Although you deserve to die, you son of a bitch
for what you did
You live
I hope you know what you gave up
The day you first put your hands on me

I might have defended myself against you
But I hate it all just the same
And I hate you for making me so angry
Just die already and save us all more misery
please
No more do I want to hear about you hurting
someone else…

Just Stop, Already

Wilted, cast out
Flowers died
Spirits of ash
I cry for you
I cannot will myself to stop
Penance for being alive
Take a soul
Take my soul
Hurt is all I feel
Useless
Unable to see
Given over
To the torturous pain
Nowhere do I see
There is no light
Darkness please
This is hell
There is no more
Stop
Let me just go
I can't see down here
Free me
Let go
Release me from this pain
Keep hurting us no more
Just stop it…

Not Even Death

A heart that drips with desire
Sits silently in the dark
Measuring her own webs in the shadows

Her hands are cold
Her heart stays warm
Even though she's alone

As the fates decreed

She sits wondering
Silently
Never to truly tell a soul

She's bent until she can bend no more
Broken, turning gray upon an ashen floor
Glass embedded in her sides

Not even death could fix her soul

Holes

In the darkness of the shadows within
I see you little by little
Riddled with holes no one else sees
The scars only appear to me

As perceptive as you seem to be
The holes, silent no longer bleeding
They remain
Your scars are forever just like mine

Damaged and broken
Even worlds apart I see it
The eyes that look upon you
They're not innocent

But did you know
In order to fix a soul
It must be done,
By the one who holds it in their own cage

It's up to you to fill those holes
I can only watch you as you do
And hope it comes to light out of shadows and
darkness
The place we dwelled too long

Burning Candles

Candles burning in the wind,
Light our path from within.
Burning deep, solidly,
Since the pain 'don't come cheap.'

Ink runs dry in unsteady hands,
Hands much, much like mine.
Shaky from the years,
Some not yet upon me outside,
Inside in the invisible void...seen.

The scars that hold us together like glue,
Never seen but always heard.
The bond that binds us,
The unbidden wreckage,
Riding upon the bloody waters of our hearts.

They say, 'In time the scars fade,'
It takes too much time,
Not enough fading.
Always inside seen,
And known to the very depths of my soul.

No ripping and breaking of the cage,
Just candles to light the way,
Back from the shadows of the past,
That will haunt us 'til forever.

Love, Pain, and Rage

Lower me to pits of hell,
Says she,
The lover, the fighter,
The one who held your heart in her hand.
What doth it mean?
To consume my very soul in the flames that burn
brighter than a thousand sunsets?
To give all I have to someone
Who knows not what it means to console inside
Yourself the very vessel
Of your own pain and rage?
Love doesn't float on angel wings
Down to your doorstep
And stop in front,
Waiting to hear the creaking of hinges on metal
scrapes.
It waits so dormant,
For the day it reveals itself
And cannot be plunged back into the box it was
taken from.
Unfortunate…very unfortunate for the ones it
traps with its spells and yearnings…

The Bridge

Built in defiance
Of what was supposed to be love
What turned to nothing quickly
Then to hate

You were supposed to be
A saving grace
Yet hollow were the intentions
Set upon you in your heart

Shallow were the vestige inside
The blood in your veins
Isn't the same as mine,
You do *not* bleed red

Devils and demons do *not* bleed
There is nothing inside
But a blackened husk
What used to be humanity is gone

Without a soul,
Who are you?
In the pit of despair
Your shadow grows

But in this world
You are no more
You cannot hurt what you didn't make
You cannot kill what isn't yours

You didn't make us
Good luck trying to break us
You're nothing more
Than a snake under the bed of this life

Devil, demon personage
You shall die
By the hands that fed you
They shall steal your worth completely

Keep burning, torching, and blowing up
The bridges of life's souls
See what happens to you
In this end of yours

The Darkness Falls

Darkness falls
It weeps
Misguided
Loving no more
Its cherished light

Upon the days
Stuck too much
In shadows
Cast out from the world
In ruin

Darkness falls
Upon us all
Stinging
Blotting us out
Hurting us

On our knees
We beg
For forgiveness
That never comes
As light fades

Cherished Days

I cherish those days
The ones I made you smile

I cherish those days
My heart didn't feel so fragile

I look back and smile
On those days when it all seemed worthwhile

To Sleep

To sleep, to dream,
Yet think of you,
My heart grows weary
As it still yearns for what it did then
To find you
And love and peace

But to sleep, then dream
Of you
Sometimes it will just have to do
Because my heart grows weary
With unrest, yes discontent
As I weep inside, yet never tell

And to sleep, to dream,
Is all there is left
My love is spent
And yet, I miss you still
Softly, I think, I always will

And so the distorted life breaks
Beating on the shore
Tearing at the vestibule of hate
Ripping at my heart
Appendages torn wide open
Bleeding emotions
Love seeping to the floor

Take Me Home

Take me home,
Where the briars live
Take me home,
A place where silence lives
Take me home,
Lay me to rest

The weary, weak, mild, and meek
Seek nothing but to silence me here
In the place where I began

Take me home,
A forgotten place
Take me home,
No more loudness
Take me home,
If only for a little while

Send out your servants to gather me up
To take me to a shining place
If such a place exists

Take me home,
Bury me on this ground
Take me home,
It's time to see you
Take me home,
Just bury me

Silence Be…

No singing, no sound, no noises abound
No birds in the distance
No barking dogs
No cars revving engines outside the window

I want nothing, I long for nothing
I hurt for peace inside me
And anger of this day to go away

Silence be, what silence is
Still motionless under glass
'Take no prisoners,' they said.
I have none nor want the need of them

I want nothing more from anything in life
Other than all I earn and what I'm able to learn
Longing only to do so with my head and my
heart

Stillness, please wash over me
Carry me to lands unknown
Silence be, what silence is
Quiet please, sitting here alone

About the author:

Jennifer Oneal Gunn was born January 2, 1979 in Carthage, Missouri. She grew up learning and knowing her imagination, it was pretty evident there was something always inside her waiting to get out. Today, Jennifer writes a plethora of different things from hard core horror that induces nightmares to soft loving poetry. Her titles include *Mystik Legends, Devil's in the Details- Reboot, Fire, Ice & Blood- The Story of Jake and Holly Book 1 (Revenging the Evil Series)*, and other numerous short stories in anthologies.

http://www.jenniferonealgunnauthor.weebly.com
https://www.facebook.com/Writer.J.Gunn.is.a.Legend
Twitter name: @WriterJGunn

www.ingramcontent.com/pod-product-compliance
Lightning Source LLC
Chambersburg PA
CBHW070640030426
42337CB00020B/4090